My First Look at French

by Jenna Lee Gleisner

toy
le jouet
(LUH joo-E)

towel
la serviette
(LA serv-IETT)

Bullfrog
Books

Ideas for Parents and Teachers

Bullfrog Books let children practice reading informational text at the earliest reading levels. Repetition, familiar words, and photo labels support early readers.

Before Reading

- Discuss the cover photo. What does it tell them?

- Read through the introduction on page 4 and book guide on page 5.

Read the Book

- "Walk" through the book and look at the photos. Let the child ask questions. Point out the photo labels. Sound out the words together.

- Read the book to the child, or have him or her read independently.

After Reading

- Prompt the child to think more. Ask: Have you heard or spoken French before? Practice saying the French words in this book.

Bulltrog Books are published by Jump!
5357 Penn Avenue South
Minneapolis, MN 55419
www.jumplibrary.com

Library of Congress Cataloging-in-Publication Data

Names: Gleisner, Jenna Lee, author.
Title: My first look at French / by Jenna Lee Gleisner.
Description: Minneapolis, MN: Jump!, Inc., [2020]
Series: First look at languages | Includes index.
Audience: Ages: 5–8
Identifiers: LCCN 2019031153 (print)
LCCN 2019031154 (ebook)
ISBN 9781645273035 (hardcover)
ISBN 9781645273042 (ebook)
Subjects: LCSH: French language—Textbooks for foreign speakers—English—Juvenile literature.
Classification: LCC PC2129.E5 G57 2020 (print) | LCC PC2129.E5 (ebook) | DDC 448.2/421—dc23
LC record available at https://lccn.loc.gov/2019031153
LC ebook record available at https://lccn.loc.gov/2019031154

Editor: Jenna Trnka
Designer: Michelle Sonnek
Translator: Anne-Sophie Seidler

Photo Credits: Vladyslav Starozhylov/Shutterstock, cover (left); nelea33/Shutterstock, cover (middle); PI/Shutterstock, cover (right); goir/Shutterstock, 1; Dima Moroz/Shutterstock, 3; Olga Popova/Shutterstock, 5; wavebreakmedia/Shutterstock, 6, 12–13, 14, 14–15; nadianb/Shutterstock, 7; New Africa/Shutterstock, 8–9, 16–17; Roman Debree/Shutterstock, 10–11; Patryk Kosmider/Shutterstock, 18; Denise Kappa/Shutterstock, 18–19; kali9/iStock, 20–21; LubaShi/Shutterstock, 24.

Printed in the United States of America at Corporate Graphics in North Mankato, Minnesota.

Table of Contents

clock
l'horloge
(L-orl-OJ)

Introduction to French

Where Is French Spoken?

French is spoken in France and many other countries around the world, including Switzerland, Belgium, Luxembourg, Canada, and some countries in Africa.

How It Differs from English

- The French language uses the same alphabet as English, but the pronunciations are quite different.

- In French, the "h" is silent.

- The French language doesn't have the "th" sound.

- Sometimes, letters in words are not pronounced, like the final "t" in petit (small) or the final "d" in placard (closet).

Marks

Marks are sometimes added above vowels or under the "c": à, â, é, è, ê, ë, î, ï, ô, ù, û, ü, ç. They change the pronunciation of the letter or the meaning of the word. For example, "ou" means "or," but "où" with an accent means "where."

You can speak French, too! Let's learn!

Book Guide

This book follows Léo during a typical day. He speaks French. We will learn what his family members, teachers, and friends are called in French. We will also learn the French words for common items we see and use every day.

There are three labels for each word. The first is the English word. The second is the French word. The third is how we pronounce, or say, it. The stressed syllable is in uppercase.

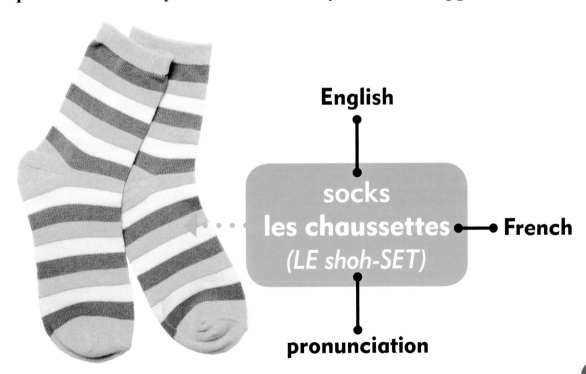

English

socks
les chaussettes → **French**
(LE shoh-SET)

pronunciation

Let's Learn French!

This is Léo.

6

He speaks French.

Let's learn!

French
le Français
(LUH fron-SE)

shirt
le t-shirt
(LUH tee-SHURT)

pants
le pantalon
(LUH pon-ta-LON)

backpack
le sac à dos
(LUH SAK-a-doh)

shoes
les chaussures
(LE shoh-SUUR)

ball
le ballon
(LUH ba-LON)

He gets ready for school.

He picks out clothes
from his closet.

closet
le placard
(LUH pla-KAR)

He eats breakfast.

Can you say toast in French?

Practice!

orange
l'orange
(LO-RAWNJ)

cereal
les céréales
(LE se-re-AL)

juice
le jus
(LUH JUU)

jam
la confiture
(LA kon-FEE-TUUR)

breakfast
le petit déjeuner
(LUH puh-TEE de-juh-NE)

toast
le pain grillé
(LUH PAH gree-YE)

11

chalkboard
le tableau
(LUH ta-BLOH)

school
l'école
(LE-KOL)

friend
l'amie
(la-MEE)

pencil
le crayon
(LUH kre-YON)

paper
le papier
(LUH pa-PEE-YE)

desk
la table
(LA TA-bluh)

Léo goes to school.

His friends are here!

His class goes to the library.

He picks out a book.

book
le livre
(LUH LEE-vruh)

bookshelf
l'étagère
(le-ta-JER)

library
la bibliothèque
(LA bee-blee-oh-TEK)

teacher
la professeure
(LA proh-fe-SUR)

student
l'élève
(LE-LEV)

floor
le sol
(LUH SOL)

15

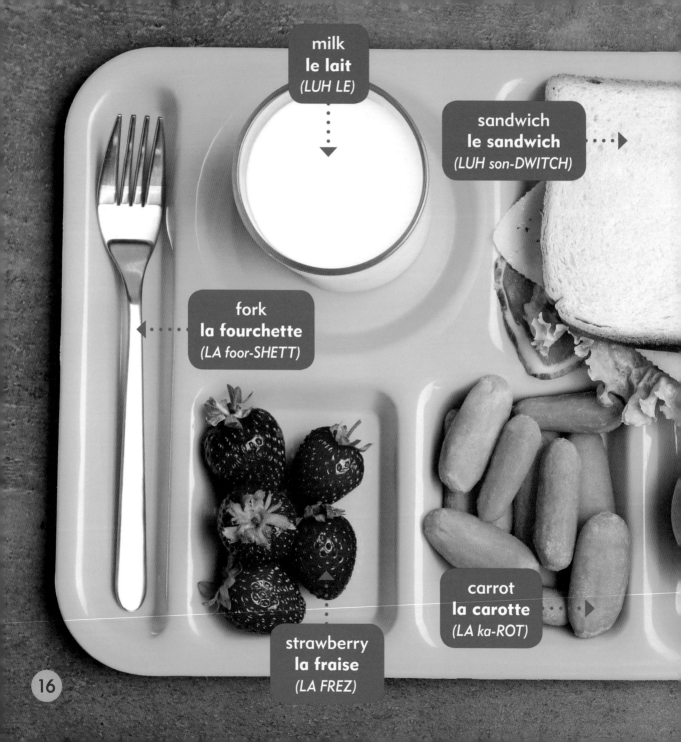

milk
le lait
(LUH LE)

sandwich
le sandwich
(LUH son-DWITCH)

fork
la fourchette
(LA foor-SHETT)

carrot
la carotte
(LA ka-ROT)

strawberry
la fraise
(LA FREZ)

16

lunch
le déjeuner
(LUH de-juh-NE)

apple
la pomme
(LA POM)

It is lunchtime.

He picks his favorite foods.

Léo walks home from school.

His dog greets him!

His name is Oreo.

dog
le chien
(LUH SHIAH)

car
la voiture
(LA vwa-TUUR)

sky
le ciel
(LUH SEE-EL)

home
la maison
(LA meh-ZON)

window
la fenêtre
(LA fuh-NE-truh)

door
la porte
(LA POR-tuh)

grass
l'herbe
(L-ERB)

19

sister
la sœur
(LA SUR)

father
le père
(LUH PERR)

brother
le frère
(LUH FRERR)

mother
la mère
(LA MERR)

family
la famille
(LA fa-MEE-yuh)

outside
à l'extérieur
(A lex-te-RI-YUHR)

His family likes
to be outside.

Fun!

21

Phrases to Know

Hello!
Bonjour!
(bon-JOOR)

Goodbye!
Au revoir!
(OH ruh-VWAR)

Yes.
Oui.
(WEE)

No.
Non.
(NON)

Thank you!
Merci!
(mer-SI)

You're welcome.
De rien.
(DUH REE-AH)

My name is _____.
Je m'appelle _____.
(JUH ma-PELL)

How are you?
Comment allez-vous?
(kom-AH-TA-le-VOO)

Colors

red **le rouge** *(LUH ROOJ)*	orange **l'orange** *(LO-RAWNJ)*	yellow **le jaune** *(LUH JOH-nuh)*	green **le vert** *(LUH VER)*	blue **le bleu** *(LUH BLUH)*
purple **le violet** *(LUH vioh-LE)*	pink **le rose** *(LUH ROHZ)*	brown **le marron** *(LUH ma-RON)*	gray **le gris** *(LUH GREE)*	black **le noir** *(LUH NWAR)*

Numbers

1 un *(UH)*	2 deux *(DUH)*	3 trois *(TRWA)*	4 quatre *(KA-truh)*	5 cinq *(SUNK)*
6 six *(SISS)*	7 sept *(SET)*	8 huit *(WEET)*	9 neuf *(NUFF)*	10 dix *(DISS)*

Index

flower
la fleur
(LA FLUHR)

To Learn More

FACT SURFER

Finding more information is as easy as 1, 2, 3.

❶ Go to www.factsurfer.com

❷ Enter "myfirstlookatFrench" into the search box.

❸ Click the "Surf" button to see a list of websites.